To Becky
with much love

from

Karen

WORDS FROM THE BIBLE ABOUT PEACE

Be Still

Edited and designed by Ben Alex

scandinavia

BE STILL
WORDS FROM THE BIBLE ABOUT PEACE

Published by Scandinavia Publishing House 2012
Scandinavia Publishing House
Drejervej 15,3, DK-2400 Copenhagen, NV
Denmark
E-mail: info@scanpublishing.dk
Web: www.scanpublishing.dk

Concept, editing and design by Ben Alex
All quotes from New International Version unless otherwise noted
Photo copyright © Dreamstime pages 2,8,10,15,18,23,24,32,40,49,
50,57,60,61,70,75,78,87,94,99,102,104,109,110,116,118,124,126
Photo copyright © Janis Zroback pages 28,37,42,69,81,90,121
Visit Janis at http://www.redbubble.com/people/paintability
Photo copyright © Blake Steele page 82

Printed in China
ISBN 978 87 7132 044 2

Be still,
and know that
I am God.

Psalm 46:10a

...that we may lead a quiet
and peaceable life in all
godliness and honesty.

1 Timothy 2:2b KJV

Peace in the

I will grant peace
in the land, and you will
lie down and no one will
make you afraid. I will remove
wild beasts from the land,
and the sword will not pass
through your country.
Leviticus 26:6

They found rich,
good pasture, and the land
was spacious, peaceful
and quiet.

1 Chronicles 4:40a

So the Levites
calmed all the people,
saying, "Be quiet, for
this day is holy..."

Nehemiah 8:11 ESV

You will see Zion as
a place of holy festivals.
You will see Jerusalem,
a city quiet and secure.

Isaiah 33:20a NLT

So all the people
of the land rejoiced:
and the city was calm.

2 Kings 11:20a

11

But you will have a son who
will be a man of peace and rest,
and I will give him rest from all his
enemies on every side.

1 Chronicles 22:9a

My people will abide
in a peaceful habitation,
in secure dwellings,
and in quiet resting places.

Isaiah 32:18 ESV

He built up
the fortified cities of Judah,
since the land was at peace.
No one was at war with him
during those years, for the LORD
gave him rest.

2 Chronicles 14:6

The desert and
the parched land will be glad;
the wilderness will rejoice
and blossom.

Isaiah 35:1

So will nations
give him honour;
kings will keep quiet
because of him.

Isaiah 52:15 BBE

Then said Hezekiah to Isaiah,
Good is the word of the Lord
which you have said.
And he said in his heart,
There will be peace and quiet
in my days.

Isaiah 39:8 BBE

So do not be afraid,
Jacob, my servant;
do not be dismayed, Israel,
says the Lord.
For I will bring you home again
from distant lands, and your children
will return from their exile.
Israel will return to a life
of peace and quiet, and
no one will terrorize them.

Jeremiah 30:10 NLT

I will give peace
and quietness unto Israel
in his days.

1 Chronicles 22:9b ASV

And the kingdom
of Jehoshaphat was at peace,
for his God had given him
rest on every side.

2 Chronicles 20:30

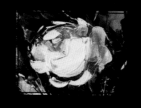

Make it your ambition
to lead a quiet life,
to mind your own business
and to work with your hands,
just as we told you.

1 Thessalonians 4:11

The Lord will make war for you,
you have only to keep quiet.

Exodus 14:14 BBE

he heart

You should stay calm
and not do anything rash.

Acts 19:36b NLT

Therefore I exhort
first of all that supplications,
prayers, intercessions, and giving of thanks
be made for all men, for kings and all
who are in authority, that we may lead
a quiet and peaceable life in all
godliness and reverence.

1 Timothy 2:1-2 NKJV

Listen in silence before me.

Isaiah 41:1a NLT

And whoso is hearkening
to me dwelleth confidently,
and is quiet from fear of evil!

Proverbs 1:33 YLT

Upon God alone
doth my soul rest peacefully;
from him is my salvation.

Psalm 62:1 DBT

The LORD is
in his holy temple.
All the earth should be
silent in his presence.

Habakkuk 2:20 GWT

Stand in silence in
the presence of the Sovereign LORD,
for the awesome day of the LORD's
judgment is near.

Zephaniah 1:7 NLT

Then they are glad
because they are quiet;
So He guides them to
their desired haven.

Psalm 107:30 NKJV

And you will be safe
because there is hope;
after looking round,
you will take your
rest in quiet.

Job 11:18 BBE

When pride comes,
there comes shame,
but wisdom is with
the quiet in spirit.

Proverbs 11:2 BBE

And He giveth rest,
and who maketh wrong?

Job 34:29 YLT

I was quiet,
and kept my mouth shut;
because you had done it.

Psalm 39:9 BBE

A wise man keeps quiet.

Proverbs 11:12b BBE

The only effect
of pride is fighting;
but wisdom is with
the quiet in spirit.

Proverbs 13:10 BBE

He who is quickly angry
will do what is foolish,
but the man of good sense
will have quiet.

Proverbs 14:17 BBE

He makes me lie
down in green pastures,
he leads me beside quiet waters.

Psalm 23:2

He who has
knowledge says little;
and he who has a calm spirit
is a man of good sense.

Proverbs 17:27 BBE

A quiet spirit
can overcome even
great mistakes.
Ecclesiastes 10:4 NLT

A quiet and

A time for keeping quiet
and a time for talk;

Ecclesiastes 3:7b BBE

You will lie down,
with no one to make you afraid,
and many will court
your favor.

Job 11:19

humble spirit

When you lie down,
you will not be afraid;
when you lie down,
your sleep will be sweet.

Proverbs 3:24 NASB

I lay down and slept,
yet I woke up in safety,
for the LORD was
watching over me.

Psalm 3:5 NLT

Be still before
the Lord and wait
patiently for Him.

Psalm 37:7a

For the one who
has entered (God's) rest
has himself also
rested from his works,
as God did from His.

Hebrews 4:10

Better a dry crust with peace
and quiet than a house full
of feasting, with strife.

Proverbs 17:1

A heart at peace
gives life to the body,
but envy rots the bones.

Proverbs 14:30

For thus said the Lord GOD,
the Holy One of Israel,
"In returning and rest you shall be saved;
in quietness and in trust shall
be your strength.

Isaiah 30:15 ESV

The whole earth
is at rest and quiet;
they break forth
into singing.

Isaiah 14:7 ESV

Make search for the Lord,
all you quiet ones of the earth,
who have done what is right in his eyes;
make search for righteousness and a quiet heart:
it may be that you will be safely covered
in the day of the Lord's wrath.

Zephaniah 2:3 BBE

Wait patiently
for the LORD.
Be brave and courageous.
Yes, wait patiently
for the LORD.

Psalm 27:14 NLT

Surely I have composed
and quieted my soul;
like a weaned child rests
against his mother.

Psalm 131:2 NASB

Let the peace of Christ rule in your hearts,
since as members of one body you were called to peace.
And be thankful.

Colossians 3:15

The rulers kept quiet,
and put their hands on their mouths;

Job 29:9 BBE

After I had said what was in my mind,
they were quiet and let my words go
deep into their hearts.

Job 29:22 BBE

One dies in his full strength,
being wholly at ease and quiet.

Job 21:23 KJV

Be careful,
keep calm and don't be afraid.
Do not lose heart.

Isaiah 7:4

If only you would keep quiet,
it would be a sign of wisdom!

Job 13:5 BBE

The words of the wise
heard in quiet are better than the cry
of him that ruleth among fools.

Ecclesiastes 9:17 ASV

47

But I will still have
among you a quiet and poor people,
and they will put their faith
in the name of the Lord.

Zephaniah 3:12 BBE

Blessed are the poor in spirit,
for theirs is the kingdom
of heaven.

Matthew 5:3

But you,
O man of God,
flee these things
and pursue righteousness,
godliness, faith, love,
patience, gentleness.

1 Timothy 6:11 NKJV

Be still in the
presence of the LORD,
and wait patiently for him to act.
Don't worry about evil people
who prosper or fret about
their wicked schemes.

Psalm 37:7 NLT

The peace

You will keep in perfect peace
him whose mind is steadfast,
because he trusts in you.

Isaiah 26:3

My soul,
wait in silence for God only,
for my hope is from Him.

Psalm 62:5

My soul within me
is like a child who
no longer nurses.

Psalm 131:2b NLV

Be still,
and know that I am God;
I will be exalted among the nations,
I will be exalted in the earth.

Psalm 46:10

Then God blessed
the seventh day and sanctified it,
because in it He rested from all His work
which God had created and made.

Genesis 2:3 NKJV

For now should I have
lain still and been quiet,
I should have slept:
then would I have
been at rest.

Job 3:13 KJV

Then a great
and powerful wind
tore the mountains apart and
shattered the rocks before the Lord,
but the Lord was not in the wind.
After the wind there was an earthquake,
but the Lord was not in the earthquake.
After the earthquake came a fire,
but the Lord was not in the fire.
And after the fire came
a gentle whisper.

1 Kings 19:11-12

There will be
silence before You.

Psalm 65:1a NASB

And he awoke
and rebuked the wind and
said to the sea, "Peace! Be still!"
And the wind ceased, and
there was a great calm.

Mark 4:39 ESV

See how the lilies of the field grow.
They do not labor or spin.

Matthew 6:28b

May the grace
of the Lord Jesus Christ,
and the love of God,
and the fellowship of the Holy Spirit
be with you all.

2 Corinthians 13:14

The grace of
the Lord Jesus be with
God's people. Amen.

Revelation 22:21

I will lie down in peace and sleep,
for you alone, O LORD, will keep me safe.

Psalm 4:8

Jesus is the

The disciples went
and woke him, saying,
"Master, Master, we're going to drown!"
He got up and rebuked the wind
and the raging waters;
the storm subsided,
and all was calm.

Luke 8:24

vay of peace

And you, my child,
will be called a prophet of the Most High;
for you will go on before the Lord
to prepare the way for him,
to give his people the knowledge of salvation
through the forgiveness of their sins,
because of the tender mercy of our God,
by which the rising sun will come to us
from heaven to shine on those living in darkness
and in the shadow of death, to guide
our feet into the path of peace.

Luke 1:76-79

Glory to God
in the highest heaven,
and on earth peace to those
on whom his favor rests.

Luke 2:14

For the Kingdom of God
is not a matter of what we eat or drink,
but of living a life of goodness and peace
and joy in the Holy Spirit.

Romans 14:17 NLT

For God was
pleased to have all
his fullness dwell in him,
and through him to reconcile
to himself all things,
whether things on earth
or things in heaven,
by making peace through
his blood, shed on the cross.

Colossians 1:19-20

But the wisdom that is from above is pure,
filled with peace, meek and attentive, filled with love
and good fruit, without division and
does not show partiality.

James 3:17 ABPE

Now such persons we command and
encourage in the Lord Jesus Christ to do
their work quietly and to earn their own living.

2 Thessalonians 3:12 NLT

Instead, it should be
that of your inner self,
the unfading beauty of a gentle
and quiet spirit, which is of
great worth in God's sight.

1 Peter 3:4

Now I, Paul, myself
make request to you by the quiet and
gentle behaviour of Christ...

2 Corinthians 10:1a BBE

nd gentle

Now those things
which were put down in writing
before our time were for our learning,
so that through quiet waiting and
through the comfort of
the holy Writings we might
have hope.

Romans 15:4 BBE

But in everything
making it clear that
we are the servants of God,
in quiet strength, in troubles,
in need, in sorrow.

2 Corinthians 6:4 BBE

But the fruit
of the Spirit is love,
joy, peace, a quiet mind,
kind acts, well-doing,
faith...

Galatians 5:22 BBE

With all gentle
and quiet behaviour,
taking whatever comes,
putting up with one
another in love...

Ephesians 4:2 BBE

And may your hearts
be guided by the Lord
into the love of God and
quiet waiting for Christ.

2 Thessalonians 3:5 BBE

That old men are
to be simple in their tastes,
serious, wise, true in faith,
in love, and of a quiet mind.

Titus 2:2 BBE

I, John, your brother, who have
a part with you in the trouble and the kingdom
and the quiet strength of Jesus....

Revelation 1:9a BBE

If any man sends others into prison,
into prison he will go; if any man puts to death
with the sword, with the sword will he be put to death.
Here is the quiet strength and
the faith of the saints.

Revelation 13:10 BBE

Here is the quiet strength
of the saints, who keep the orders of God,
and the faith of Jesus.

Revelation 14:12 BBE

Come to me, all who are tired from
carrying heavy loads, and I will give you rest.

Matthew 11:28 GWT

God has told his people,
"Here is a place of rest;
let the weary rest here.
This is a place of quiet rest."

Isaiah 28:12 NLT

The LORD gives strength to his people;
the LORD blesses his people with peace.

Psalm 29:11

For I am
the Lord your God,
who makes the sea calm
when its waves are
thundering.

Isaiah 51:15 BBE

You rule
the pride of the sea.
When its waves rise up,
you calm them.

Psalms 89:9 HNV

I will be calm
and will not be angry
with you anymore.

Ezekiel 16:42b NLT

O LORD,
you know all about this.
Do not stay silent.

Psalm 35:22 NLT

This is what the LORD says to me:
"I will remain quiet and will look on
from my dwelling place, like shimmering heat
in the sunshine, like a cloud of dew
in the heat of harvest."

Isaiah 18:4

He will rejoice
over you with joy.
He will calm you in his love.
He will rejoice over
you with singing.

Zephaniah 3:17 WEB

And after the earthquake a fire;
but the LORD was not in the fire:
and after the fire a still small voice.

1 Kings 19:12 WBT

And self-control to knowledge,
and a quiet mind to self-control,
and fear of God to a quiet mind...

2 Peter 1:6 BBE

Let the peace of
Christ rule in your hearts,
since as members of one body
you were called to peace.
And be thankful.

Colossians 3:15

The LORD is my shepherd, I lack nothing.
He makes me lie down in green pastures,
he leads me beside quiet waters, he refreshes my soul.
He guides me along the right paths for his name's sake.
Even though I walk through the darkest valley,
I will fear no evil, for you are with me;
your rod and your staff, they comfort me.

You prepare a table before me
in the presence of my enemies.
You anoint my head with oil; my cup overflows.
Surely your goodness and love will follow me
all the days of my life,
and I will dwell in the house of the LORD forever.

Psalm 23

Jesus said to the woman,
"You are saved because you believed.
Go in peace."

Luke 7:50

The fruit of
righteousness will be peace;
the effect of righteousness
will be quietness and
confidence forever.

Isaiah 32:17

And those who are peacemakers
will plant seeds of peace and reap
a harvest of righteousness.

James 3:18 NLT

The grace of
our Lord Jesus Christ
be with your spirit,
brothers and sisters.
Amen.

Galatians 6:18

Being glad in hope,
quiet in trouble,
at all times given to prayer.

Romans 12:12 BBE

No discipline is enjoyable
while it is happening – it's painful!
But afterward there will be a peaceful harvest
of right living for those who are
trained in this way.

Hebrews 12:11 NLT

Then Jacob was left alone.
And a man fought with him
until morning.

Genesis 32:24

One day Jesus went up
on a mountain to pray.
He prayed all night to God.

Luke 6:12

And when it was day,
he departed and went into
a desolate place.

Luke 4:42a ESV

till

Be still before the Lord,
all mankind, because he has roused himself
from his holy dwelling.

Zechariah 2:13

103

By his power
the sea was made quiet.

Job 26:12 BBE

I have set my face
toward the earth,
and have been silent...

Daniel 10:15 YLT

May the LORD silence
all flattering lips and every
boastful tongue.

Psalm 12:3a

Let their lying lips be silenced,
for with pride and contempt they speak
arrogantly against the righteous.

Psalm 31:18

No man will be able to stand
against you all the days of your life.
I will be with you just as I have been with Moses.
I will be faithful to you and will
not leave you alone.

Joshua 1:5

My presence
will go with you,
and I will give
you rest.

Exodus 33:14

Live in harmony with one another.
Do not be proud, but be willing to associate
with people of low position.
Do not be conceited.

Romans 12:16

Jesus went from there and came to the Sea of Galilee.
Then He went up the mountain and sat down.

Matthew 15:29

When he rose from prayer
and went back to the disciples,
he found them asleep,
exhausted from sorrow.

Luke 22:45

Do all that you can
to live in peace with everyone.

Romans 12:18 NLT

Finally, brothers, good-by.
Aim for perfection, listen to my appeal,
be of one mind, live in peace.
And the God of love and peace
will be with you.

2 Corinthians 13:11

peace

And so, dear friends,
while you are waiting for
these things to happen,
make every effort to be found
living peaceful lives that are pure
and blameless in his sight.

2 Peter 3:14 NLT

Salt is excellent,
but if salt becomes tasteless,
with what shall it be seasoned?
Have salt in you and be at peace
with one another.

Mark 9:50 ABPE

So it is good to wait quietly
for salvation from the Lord.

Lamentations 3:26 NLT

Though the mountains
be shaken and the hills
be removed, yet my unfailing love
for you will not be shaken
nor my covenant of peace
be removed," says the LORD,
who has compassion on you.

Isaiah 54:10

119

Hold them in
the highest regard
in love because of their work.
Live in peace with
each other.

1 Thessalonians 5:13

I am writing
to Timothy, my dear son.
May God the Father and
Christ Jesus our Lord
give you grace, mercy,
and peace.

2 Timothy 1:2 NLT

Jesus said to them again,
"Peace be with you.
As the Father has sent me,
even so I am sending you."

John 20:21 ESV

I am leaving you with a gift –
peace of mind and heart.
And the peace I give is a gift
the world cannot give.
So don't be troubled or afraid.

John 14:27 NLT

with you

124

I have told you these things,
so that in me you may have peace.
In this world you will have trouble.
But take heart! I have overcome the world.

John 16:33

Very early in the morning,
while it was still dark, Jesus got up,
left the house and went off to
a solitary place, where he prayed.

Mark 1:35

But Jesus often withdrew
to lonely places and prayed.

Luke 5:16

As soon as Jesus heard the news,
he left in a boat to a remote area to be alone.

Matthew 14:13 NLT

When I was waiting
quietly for the Lord,
his heart was turned to me,
and he gave ear to my cry.

Psalms 40:1 BBE

Let those who are happy
when I am declared innocent
joyfully sing and rejoice.
Let them continually say,
"The LORD is great. He is happy when
his servant has peace."

Psalm 35:27 GWT